LINES
SCRIBBLED
ON AN
ENVELOPE

and other poems

LINES
SCRIBBLED
ON AN
ENVELOPE

and other poems

by

MADELEINE
L'ENGLE

FARRAR, STRAUS

& GIROUX

New York

811

For

MADELEINE

SAUNDERS

JONES

PREFACE

Poetry, at least the kind I write, is written out of immediate
need; it is written out of pain, joy, and experience too great to
be borne until it is ordered into words. And then it is written
to be shared. If something has happened to me, and I am
driven to express it in particular words, then perhaps my
experience will awaken a response in others who have had like
experiences: so I have sent my verses out across the country
in letters. I have a vast and varied and happy correspondence,
and lots of it has come through people who have written to
me because they have heard me speak, or read one of my
books. And over and over again they have written to me, "Your
poems mean so much to me. When are they going to be put
in a book?"

The poems mean a great deal to me, too. So why am I
hesitant about this book? Perhaps because I am afraid of
making myself vulnerable to people I don't know. And then I
remember hearing a writer say: "Just as we have suffered
terribly from the sexual repression of the Victorian age, so
we are already beginning to suffer from the spiritual repression
of the past decades." Is it only because I live in a modern
Babylon that I am so aware that to talk of the things of the
spirit is embarrassing to most people? It really isn't done by
anybody except the lame, the halt, and the blind, poor things,
who are to be pitied because it's all they have.

And then I remember a conversation I had with a high
school senior who was a member of a creative writing seminar
I was teaching. We had come a long way together; she had
a lot against her, though she was brilliant. But she had a
beautiful and domineering mother who made her feel unlovely
and inadequate; she was black; she was in constant difficulties
with the authorities at school. But we had come to be good
friends who could talk, usually, and late one afternoon after
our seminar she was walking me home with a group of other
girls and boys. One of them said something about seeing me
Sunday in church, and she stopped in shock and disbelief.

"But you don't mean you're a Christian!"

"Struggling to be."

"But you don't mean you go to church?"

"Yes."

She thought this over. "Oh, well, I suppose when you grow
old and near death then probably you need it to keep you
from being afraid."

My response to this was spontaneous and rather raucous
laughter. This is about the reverse of the real thing. Not to
mention the fact that I'm not yet an antique—though I
remember from my own youth that there wasn't much
difference in my mind between thirty and sixty. We then
proceeded to have a good talk, over several pots of tea and a

vast number of cookies, and when we were done there was still distance between our viewpoints, but the distance was a lot smaller.

If my response hadn't been hilarity, followed by conversation, then perhaps our ability to communicate would have been ended. And it wasn't easy for me to talk to this girl about all the things I talk about in the poems. But I'm glad I did. We both learned.

It takes courage to be open and vulnerable, and if it took courage to be open and vulnerable with her, it perhaps takes even more to send out a selection of these lines "scribbled on envelopes."

M. L'E.

CONTENTS

LINES
SCRIBBLED
ON AN
ENVELOPE

and other poems

T O   A

LONG-LOVED LOVE

(i)

We, who have seen the new moon grow old together,
Who have seen winter rime the fields and stones
As though it would claim earth and water forever,
We who have known the touch of flesh and the shape of
    bones
Know the old moon stretching its shadows across a whitened
    field
More beautiful than spring with all its spate of blooms;
What passion knowledge of tried flesh still yields,
What joy and comfort these familiar rooms.

(ii)

In the moonless, lampless dark now of this bed
My body knows each line and curve of yours;
My fingers know the shape of limb and head:
As pure as mathematics ecstasy endures.
Blinded by night and love we share our passion,
Certain of burning flesh, of living bone:
So feels the sculptor in the moment of creation
Moving his hands across the uncut stone.

(iii)

I know why a star gives light
Shining quietly in the night;

Arithmetic helps me unravel
The hours and years this light must travel
To penetrate our atmosphere.
I can count the craters on the moon
With telescopes to make them clear.
With delicate instruments I can measure
The secrets of barometric pressure.

And therefore I find it inexpressibly queer
That with my own soul I am out of tune,
And that I have not stumbled on the art
Of forecasting the weather of the heart.

My father gives me everything
I ask for. Don't you envy me?
I swim faster than a bird can wing.
Sea gulls cannot catch me: see?
Who else has hair of silk sea green?
Or silver scales, shining, alive?
My father's king (there is no queen).
I can dive full fathom five.

You wonder why I never cry?
Why mermaids have no need for tears?
Upon my sea-salt rock I lie
And play with time and laugh at years
And send my song along the air
And sing my call to passing ships,
And there is nothing quite so fair
As the cold touch of dead men's lips.

My father gives me everything,
Gold and frankincense and mer-
Boys for my sport. I lie and sing.
A sailor shouts, "Don't look at her!"
I lie upon my sea-swept stone
And wait. The sailor hears and cries.

More bleached white bones to call my own
And his salt tears before he dies.

My father gives me everything.

That's just sea water in my eyes.

LINES SCRIBBLED
ON AN ENVELOPE
WHILE RIDING
THE 104
BROADWAY BUS:

There is too much pain
I cannot understand
I cannot pray

I cannot pray for all the little ones with bellies bloated by
    starvation in India;
for all the angry Africans striving to be separate in a world
    struggling for wholeness;
for all the young Chinese men and women taught that
    hatred and killing are good and compassion evil;
or even all the frightened people in my own city looking
    for truth in pot or acid.

Here I am
and the ugly man with beery breath beside me reminds me
    that it is not my prayers that waken your concern, my
    Lord;
my prayers, my intercessions are not to ask for your love
for all your lost and lonely ones,
your sick and sinning souls,
but mine, my love, my acceptance of your love.
Your love for the woman sticking her umbrella and her
    expensive
parcels into my ribs and snarling, "Why don't you watch
    where you're going?"

Your love for the long-haired, gum-chewing boy who shoves
    the old lady aside to grab a seat,
Your love for me, too, too tired to look with love,
too tired to look at Love, at you, in every person on the
    bus.
Expand my love, Lord, so I can help to bear the pain,
help your love move my love into the tired prostitute with
    false eyelashes and bunioned feet,
the corrupt policeman with his hand open for graft,
the addict, the derelict, the woman in the mink coat and
    discontented mouth,
the high school girl with heavy books and frightened eyes.

Help me through these scandalous particulars
to understand
your love.

Help me to pray.

O sing unto God
and sing praises unto his Name
magnify him that rideth upon the heavens
praise him in his Name
Jah!
shout it
cry it aloud upon the wind
take the tail of his steed
and fling across the sky
in his wild wake
Jah!
he cannot be caught
he cannot be fled
he cannot be known
nor his knowledge escaped
the light of his Name
blinds the brilliance of stars
Jah!
catch the falling dragon
ride between his flailing wings
leap between the jaws of the lion
grasp the horn of the unicorn
calling with mighty voice
Jah!

caught in star flame
whipped by comet lash
rejoice before him
cry above the voices of the cherubim
shout alongside the seraphim
Jah!
bellow joy behind kings
scattered by the quaking of his hills
fleeing before his fire
rush like snow through his thunderous flame
crying with gladness
adoration of his Name
God is Lord
Jah!

BODY,
THE BLACK HORSE
AND THE WHITE

Body, the black horse and the white,
Who bears me through the day and night,
How shall I ride when you are gone?
Without my steed am I undone?
Black horse and white, O wingèd horse,
Sinister, dextrous, holding course,
O wingèd horse with single horn,
O Pegasus, O unicorn,
Body my body, when you're in grave
Will I have any soul to save?
Body, our journey's just begun,
And rider, ridden, are only one.
How can I see your rank corruption
Except as journey's interruption?
Where am I going? How can I travel
Without my body? Truth: unravel:
Body, as dark as starless night,
Tell me, where comes the blinding light?
Body it is whose ears have heard
The thunder crashing of the Word.
The lightning flash reveals what face?
Where are we going? To what place?
How shall I ride when you are done?
How shall I once again be one?

MEDUSA

*(Because she had angered the gods, Medusa
was the only one of the Gorgons who
was not immortal.)*

I, of all Gorgons, I, alone, must die.
Since death must come to me I carry death
At all times in my face, my bitter eye.
If every breath I draw is mortal breath
Leading irrevocably to my end
I'll give stone death to all who see my face,
My span of life resentfully will spend
Denying life: revenge for my disgrace.
I, who should be immortal, have been shamed,
But cloak my shame in serpent hissing pride.
Immortal privilege denied, self maimed,
Only this arrogance can fury hide.
Think you I like the snakes upon my head?
My only pleasure is in luring men
To look, to turn to granite, silent, dead.
Then what's their use? The worst is when
Gods look on me and laugh. But look you, mortal,
I'll blast you through death's icy portal.
Thus in your death my own have I delayed.
Not god, not human—Medusa is afraid.

If thou couldst empty self of selfishness
And then with love reach out in wide embrace
Then might God come this purer self to bless;
So might thou feel the wisdom of His Grace,
And see, thereby, the radiance of His face.

But selfishness turns inwards, miry, black,
Refuses stars, sees only clouded night,
Too full, too dark, cannot confess a lack,
Turns from God's face, blest, holy, bright,
Is blinded by the presence of the Light.

THE UNICORN

(The unicorn is an untamed beast who always eludes the pursuit of hunters—unless he sees a young virgin. Then he will lie down with his head in her lap and can be easily taken.)

I am feral, free, untame,
So wild I do not have a name.
One-horn, you say? That's what I am,
But who I am I cannot tell,
For I am only that I am.
My neigh is like a forest knell
And you will never know the rapture
Of my swift flight, eluding capture.

I am not young, nor grow I old.
My heart beats softly, quiet, cold,
Is moved by no one: woman, man.
My veins are ice.
                    Wait!
                            Who goes there?
My heart stopped for a frightened span.
What is this tension in the air?
Oh, girl, not woman, more than child,
Which of us two is the more wild?

So quietly you sit and wait.
Wait: why? For whom? Am I too late?
I do not know what joy this is.

The blood runs in me like the sap.
I come to you in freedom. This
Is bliss, my head upon your lap.
Nothing will ever be the same.
Someone: tell me! What's my name?

Towards afternoon the train pulled in to the station.

The light came grey and cold through the dirty glass of the
terminal roof,

and passengers waiting on the platform blew upon their
hands and stamped their feet

and their breath came out like smoke.

In the comfortable compartment I leaned back against the
red plush of the seat

and looked out the window. All the signs were in a
language I could not read.

I got out my passport and held it, waiting in readiness.

My papers were in order and the train was warm.

The conductor slid open the door to the compartment and
said to me,

"This is your last stop on this train. You will have to get
out."

I held out my passport, "No, no, my journey's barely half
over,"

and I told him the cities through which the train was going
to pass.

He handed me back my passport and said again, "You will
have to get out,"

and he took me by the arms and led me from the coach.

His hands were so strong
     my arms cried out in pain. On the platform it was cold.
"But I don't know where I am!" I cried, "or where I am
     going."
"Follow me," he said. "I have been sent to show you."
Through the glass of the station roof I could see the sun
     was going down
and a horror of great darkness fell upon me.
"Come," the conductor said. "This is the way you are to
     go,"
and he led me past the passengers waiting on the platform
and past the foreign signs and a burning lamp in this land
where I was a stranger. He led me to a train with no lights
     and broken windows
and a pale wisp of smoke lifting from a rusty engine, and
     said,
"Get in. This is your train."
I fell upon my face and laughed and said, "But this train
     isn't going anywhere,"
and he said, "You may sit down," and I sat on a wooden
     bench
and he put my satchel on the rack over my head.
"Are you ready for the journey?" he asked me. "I must have
     your passport."

I gave it to him. "Where are we going?" I asked. The train
    was cold.
"The way will be shown," he said, and closed the
    compartment door.
I heard a puff of steam. The old engine began to pull the
    dark car
and we ventured out into the night.

You promised
well, actually you didn't promise very much, did you?
but that little is enough
is more than enough.
We fail you
over and over again
but you promised to be faithful to us
not to let us fail
beyond your forgiveness of our failure.
In our common temptation
you promised
we would not be tempted more than we are able
you promised not to lead us into temptation
beyond our frail strength
and you
yourself
are our refuge in temptation
our escape from the pit
and that is enough
so that we can bear
more than we thought we could bear
of loneliness, nothingness, otherness,
sin, silliness, sadness.
For thine is the kingdom and the other great fors:

forbearance, forgiveness,
fortitude,
forever:
this is what you promised
it is enough
it is everything.

I went into a building called a church.
A lot of monkeys sat in all the pews
and at the altar there were other monkeys
dressed in fancy clothes.
Everybody was very busy. The monkeys kept kneeling
and crossing themselves and some of them
kept looking around to see that they did everything
the other monkeys did, and maybe a little more.
They went up to the altar and their palms were pressed
    together
so that they looked very holy and they ate and drank
and the monkeys at the altar said some gibberish
and the air rang with the monkery and mockery
of words repeated until the fragment of an echo
was all that could be heard of what had once been said.

Afterwards the monkeys all shook hands and showed their
    teeth
and drank coffee to break their pious fast
and some scratched each other's backs and others
scratched at monkeys who weren't there
and all the monkeys looked around to see
if they were talking to the most important monkeys
so nobody listened to anybody else.

I went home and looked into the mirror
and raised a prehensile finger to scratch behind
my simian ear. Oh, God. O God:
where is your image?

O God
I will do thy will.
I will
to do thy will.

How can my will
will to do thy will?
If I will
to know thy will
then I fall on my own will.
How can I will
to love or to obey?
My very willing bars the way.
Willingness becomes self-will.

O God
if thou will
turn my will to thy will
if thou will
tell me thy will
it will
be in spite of
not because of
my will.

Help me to lose my will.
Each day
let my will die
so will I
be born.
New born will I live
willingly   lovingly
and will
will be no more

will be thine
O God
if thou will.

I build my house of shining glass
of crystal
prisms
light, clear,
delicate.
The wind blows
Sets my rooms to singing.
The sun's bright rays
are not held back
but pour
their radiance through the rooms
in sparkles of delight.

And what, you ask, of rain
that leaves blurred muddy streaks
across translucent purity?
What, you ask,
of the throwers of stones?

Glass shatters,
breaks,
sharp fragments pierce my flesh,
darken with blood.
The wind tinkles brittle splinters

of shivered crystal.
The stones crash through.

But never mind.
My house
My lovely shining
fragile broken house
is filled with flowers
and founded on a rock.

THE PHOENIX

*(There are many and varying legends about
the beautiful gold and scarlet bird, the
Phoenix. One is that he returns to Heliopolis
every five hundred years, and that he is born
again out of his own ashes.)*

Vulnerability is my only armour.
I, the colour of fire, of blazing sun,
A blare of yellow and gold, and not a murmur
Of feathers of grey or brown, how can I run

From friend or foe? How could I ever hide?
I shall fly freely across the threatening sky
And I shall sing. Call it, if you like, pride.
I call it joy. Perhaps it's love. My eye

Is moist with all that brings it such delight.
I love this city thronging with the day,
And all the shadows crowding in the night.
Five hundred years since I have been this way,

O city full of children, wise men, fools,
Laughter and love, and hatred, scheming, murder,
Starvation among gluttons, brothels, schools;
I fly above the city and bring order

Out of this chaos. O small hungry child
Put up your bow, put down the piercing arrow
So that your hands may still be undefiled.
All through the city I must cleanse and harrow.

Aaaaagh! I am wounded by a hunter's spear.
Against the earth my dying body crashes.
The child who did not shoot me wails in fear.
Hot on my golden feathers swift blood gushes.

Blood stains the faggots of the funeral pyre.
My eyes grow dim among the flames' wild flashes.
The child is weeping still; the flames burn higher.
Hush. I shall be born from these dead ashes.

Come.
  When?
Now. This way. I will guide you.
  Wait! Not so fast.
Hurry. You. I said you.
  Who am I?
Certainly I will be with thee.
  Is nothing, then, what it is? I had rather the rod had
  stayed a rod and not become a serpent.
Come. Quickly. While the blast of my breath opens the sea.
  Stop. I'm thirsty.
Drink water from this rock.
  But the rock moves on before us.
Go with it and drink.
  I'm tired. Can't you stop for a while?
You have already tarried too long.
  But if I am to follow you I must know your name.
I will be that I will be.
  You have set the mountain on fire.
Come. Climb.
  I will be lost in the terror of your cloud.
You are stiff-necked and of a stiff-necked people.
  YOUR people, Lord,
Indubitably.

Your wrath waxes hot. I burn.
Thus to become great.
Show me then thy glory.
No man may see my face and live. But I will cover you with my hand while I pass by.
My people turn away and cry because the skin of my face shines.
Did you not expect this?
I cannot enter the tent of the congregation because your cloud covers it and your glory fills the tabernacle. Look.
It moves before us again. Can you not stay still?
Come. Follow.
But this river is death. The waters are dark and deep.
Swim.
Now will I see your face? Where are you taking me now?
Up the mountain with me before I die.
But death
bursts into light.
Then death is
what it will be.
These men: they want to keep us here in three tabernacles. But the cloud moves. The water springs from a rock that journeys on.
You are contained in me.

But how can we contain you in ark or tabernacle or
You cannot.
Where, then?
In your heart. Come.
Still?
I will be with thee.
Who am I?
You are that I will be. Come.

Pain is a bubble in the strange, stretched skin of time,
Not time itself, it presses harshly outside familiar
    chronology
Yet is surrounded by time, trapped far from the bliss of
    eternity.

But within this austere emptiness filled only by the
    anguished stab,
Eternity's touch ministers. Listen in this music-bereft hole:
His voice comes even here. There is no place or non-place
    left without his Word.

Sometimes to listen is part of the pain, is pulling the hurt
    through the dark
Not by one's own strength, but his. The cry for help is
    heard
Though it is hard to hear the hearing. Pain is borne by the
    bearing of the Word.

It is
again
the actor's nightmare
the recurring dream:
I am waiting in the wings
and I don't know my lines:
not only that,
I don't even know what rôle I am supposed to act
or what the play is about.
It's a large cast, and evidently a costume play
but I can't figure out the period:
there seem to be costumes from all centuries.
The curtain is up and the audience attentive
in the darkness
and I don't know any of my cues:
how can I tell when to make my entrance?
Everybody else is terribly busy, and people are saying
different lines simultaneously
so I really can't get the gist of the play.
There is one actor who moves quietly
instead of milling about
as though he,
of all the company,
understands the script

and has learned his lines and actions.
Perhaps if I go on stage and follow him . . .

But now everybody is after him;
they're all surrounding him
and shouting
they have him down on the stage
and the ground cloth is dusty and dirty

this isn't a proper play at all

the audience is clapping and shouting

and he lies there on the stage
his arms spread out

what are they doing?
they have a hammer and nails

wait

this is supposed to be a play
you're not supposed to hurt the actors
you're not supposed to kill the lead
where is the author?

stop them   somebody   stop them

where is the director?
where is the producer?

let me wake up
I don't want it to be real

it's just a play
people aren't like that

are we?

FOR DANA:
4TH NOVEMBER

The end of the year is here. We are at a new beginning.
A birth has come, and we reenact
At its remembrance the extraordinary fact
Of our unique, incomprehensible being.

The new year has started, for moving and growing.
The child's laugh within and through the adult's tears,
In joy and incomprehension at the singing years
Pushes us into fresh life, new knowing.

Here at the end of the year comes the year's springing.
The falling and melting snow meet in the stream
That flows with living waters and cleanses the dream.
The reed bends and endures and sees the dove's winging.

Move into the year and the new time's turning
Open and vulnerable and loving and steady.
The stars are aflame; creation is ready.
The day is at hand: the bright sun burns.

THE ROC

*(The roc is a fabulous bird of Arabia, so huge
it can carry several large beasts at a time
to take home to feed its young.)*

Hushabye, darlings, mama'll get dinner
So sweet little fledglings won't get any thinner.
    Rockabye, rocklings, roc, roc, roc a bye.

Spiders bring squiggly worms, small as your eyelash.
Salmon catch minnows, quick as a fly flash.
    Hairy red spiders give spiderlets lice.
    Cats bring their kittens home little grey mice.
Dogs bring their puppy dogs scraps from the table.
Howling hyenas steal what they are able.
    Rockabye, rocklings, roc, roc, roc a bye.

Monkeys to monklings say, "Breakfast, mañana,
Here, catch a coconut, peel a banana."
    Rhinoceros calves eat ostriches' eggs.
    Lion cubs squabble o'er antelope legs.
Mama and papa ahunting will go
O'er valleys of diamonds and moonscapes of snow.
    Rockabye, rocklings, roc, roc, roc a bye.

Ah, now I see them, look, rocklings, my word!
I'll bring you dinner right out of that herd.
    Pachyderms flee at the sight of a flock
    Of us terrible-taloned and talented roc,

But the only meal of suitable elegance
For a flock of young roc is a handful of elephants.
  Rockabye, rocklings, roc, roc, roc a bye.

The sky is strung with glory.
Light threads from star to star
from sun to sun
a living harp.
I rejoice, I sing, I leap upwards to play.
The music is in light.
My fingers pluck the vibrant strings;
the notes pulse, throb, in exultant harmony;
I beat my wings against the strands
that reach across the galaxies
I play

NO

It is not I who play
it is the music
the music plays itself
is played
plays me
small part of an innumerable
unnumberable
orchestra.
I am flung from note to note
impaled on melody

my wings are caught on throbbing filaments of light
the wild cords cut my pinions
my arms are stretched
are bound by ropes of counterpoint
I am cross-eagled on the singing that is strung
from pulsing star
to flaming sun
to

I burn in a blaze of song.

Hold me against the dark: I am afraid.
Circle me with your arms. I am made
So tiny and my atoms so unstable
That at any moment I may explode. I am unable
To contain myself in unity. My outlines shiver
With the shock of living. I endeavor
To hold the *I* as one only for the cloud
Of which I am a fragment, yet to which I'm vowed
To be responsible. Its light against my face
Reveals the witness of the stars, each in its place
Singing, each compassed by the rest,
The many joined to one, the mightiest to the least.
It is so great a thing to be an infinitesimal part
Of this immeasurable orchestra the music bursts the heart,
And from this tiny plosion all the fragments join:
Joy orders the disunity until the song is one.

Throw out the bath water.
Never mind the baby.
The water's dark and dirty
and if we toss it maybe
we'll learn to come to terms
with the viruses and germs
that are thinning out our ranks.

Throw out the bath water
never mind the baby
I think he's dead already;
at least he's been forgotten.
The water's rank and rotten
and you won't get any thanks
if you rock the sinking boat
so steady, lads, steady
if you hope to keep afloat

throw out the bath water.
Who ever is the baby?
He's nothing but a little lamb
who thinks he is and that I am.
Catch him, catch him if you're able,
serve him up upon the table,

catch and kill the little lamb,
garnish him and make him nice:
he'll do for a sacrifice.

Throw out the bath water.
Who is this tiny baby?
Just an infant, meek and mild,
just a feeble, human child,
dying quickly, if not dead:
he won't turn your stones to bread
(serve the lamb. We must be fed).
Moving surely through the gloom
on the path from womb to tomb
this babe can't help so throw him out
otherwise he'll waken doubt.

Throw out the bath water
never mind the baby
throw the water   watch it flood
in the mingling of the blood

throw out the bath water
who is this tiny baby?
nothing but   run for your life!

the babe is sharpening the knife
his army crashes through the sea
with angry banners. Run, oh, flee,
the trumpet blasts its brilliant notes
blown by wild and heavenly hosts
the red bath water's closing tide
will swallow all who do not hide

throw out the bath water
who is this tiny baby?
The Lord strong and mighty
even the Lord mighty in battle

run from the bath water
the Lord's alarum is sounded
run from the great avenging power
O circled, cornered, utterly surrounded
there is no place to hide or cower

throw out the
run
the king of glory's coming in
who is this
even the Lord of hosts
He is the tiny baby.

Boy! little boy!

You're going to board that ship? You dare?
To go beyond the sight of land?
They've warned you, boy? If not, beware
Of me. Beware of leaving sand

For sea. Beware of that sharp ledge
That marks the boundary of the world.
If your ship topples off the edge
I'm waiting there, my coils uncurled,

My tails athrash, my eyes afire,
My head wreathed in a flashing nimbus.
      What?
How dare you say that I'm a liar?
How dare you say that word: Columbus!

How dare your ship sail and not drop
When it encounters the horizon?
I wait forever for the plop
Of falling ships; I keep my eyes on

The line where sea stops at the sky,
But nothing falls: the sailing ship
Goes round and round and round and round,
A circumnavigating trip.

For land and sea are charted now;
None think of me; I am not missed.
And none can even tell you how
I talk when I do not exist.

If this round world were only square,
If this curved earth were only flat,
You'd find that I'd be waiting there,
A monster to be frightened at.

When I was very little my father
used to toss me up in the air
and I would laugh and crow with delight
knowing that his outstretched arms
were there to receive me, that he would
never let me fall.

You have thrown me up into the coldness
beyond the galaxies. Your wild wind
blows me. Where are your hands
to catch me as I fall?

When I was very little my father
would sometimes come sit with me
at tea time. We had a game. Carefully
I would eat my egg out of its shell
and then put the shell, upside down, back
in the egg cup, and he, ferocious, would
say, "Eat your egg at once!" and together
we would open it and laugh in joy
at the empty shell.

Why has the egg turned to a
scorpion in my hand?

When I was very little my father
took me to watch the fishermen
pull in their nets leaping with silver
and he told me stories of whales and other
great fish and of ships and storms and of those
who were fishers of men.

Why is the serpent allowed to continue
spitting seductive poison in my ear?

When I was very little my father
would sometimes come in the splendor
of his white tie and tails to say me good-night
and he would let me hold the silkiness
of his top hat. He had one that
opened and shut with a sound like a shot
and this was laughter and joy, and when he left
there was always a crack of light
to shine through the bedroom door.

O father of all fathers
who takes from me the strength of words
and the comfort of images
I am alone in the dark and afraid

THE BIRTH OF
LOVE

To learn to love
is to be stripped of all love
until you are wholly without love
because
until you have gone
naked and afraid
into this cold dark place
where all love is taken from you
you will not know
that you are wholly within love.

My son goes down in the orchard to incinerate
Burning the day's trash, the accumulation
Of old letters, empty toilet-paper rolls, a paper plate,
Marketing lists, discarded manuscript, on occasion
Used cartons of bird seed, dog biscuit. The fire
Rises and sinks; he stirs the ashes till the flames expire.

Burn, too, old sins, bedraggled virtues, tarnished
Dreams, remembered unrealities, the gross
Should-haves, would-haves, the unvarnished
Errors of the day, burn, burn the loss
Of intentions, recurring failures, turn
Them all to ash. Incinerate the dross. Burn. Burn.

Never have we had it so hot.
The children turn on hydrants
and the gutters run with sweat and garbage
and blood from the stupid sullen
so-called law that is only brutes
who feel the heat, too, I suppose,
and suffer as we, being, like us, flesh.
In the dark rats run over comfortless beds
and vermin crawl across the kitchen tables
and both come out on the street
and talk hate, stirring us up
like the putrid breeze
and anger begins to stir in our sluggish veins
and so we hate. We hate and are hungry for blood.
Never have we had it so hot.
One night a man came, stinking with sweat
like the rest of us, but different,
appearing, it seemed, from nowhere,
not out of the woodwork like the others.
So, for nothing better to do, we followed him
up three flights of urine-stinking stairs
to a room hot with many lights
and bodies crowded too close together.
I found no place to sit

but by then I was curious
and what else was there to do?
I climbed over steaming bodies
and found a seat on a paint-peeling sill
of an open window. He'd been talking awhile,
the man. I came in the middle
like walking into a movie and trying to guess
what must have gone on in the beginning
and missing things because of not knowing
what went on before. Why did I stay to listen?
He was ugly and I couldn't figure his angle.
He talked about some other man he loved
and when I jeered somebody said: shut up.
So I just stayed there in the open window.
I was tired and groggy from heat, and so I fell,
first asleep, and then, as he was long talking,
right out the sooty window, three floors down
onto the street. Well, it killed me:
I'm not kidding. I was dead. Then this man
rushed down the stairs, they tell me,
and they were crowding around me and shouting
and someone said call an ambulance,
and someone else (wanting a fight) said call the cops
and this man pushed his way through the mob

and flung himself on me and held me in his arms
close and warm, and told them not to worry
(though nobody gave a damn, it was just
something to get noisy about).
Then I sat up as though I had been asleep
and all I felt was hungry
so I walked back up those three putrid flights
of stairs and someone found some bread and cheese
and I ate, and drank some wine
and someone talked about the other men, the one
I'd jeered about, and then another guy called Lazarus,
and I didn't understand. I only knew
there was a difference in the room and if we went
back on the streets on stifling nights and listened
to the screams of *hate* and *kill*
there'd be no answering fury in my blood.
There was another way somewhere for me to find,
and this squat, ugly man,
talking amidst the filth, was showing me
although I didn't understand.
We talked a long while, even till break of day,
and then he went. And I was made alive
and not a little comforted.

I, who live by words, am wordless when
I try my words in prayer. All language turns
To silence. Prayer will take my words and then
Reveal their emptiness. The stilled voice learns
To hold its peace, to listen with the heart
To silence that is joy, is adoration.
The self is shattered, all words torn apart
In this strange patterned time of contemplation
That, in time, breaks time, breaks words, breaks me,
And then, in silence, leaves me healed and mended.
I leave, returned to language, for I see
Through words, even when all words are ended.
   I, who live by words, am wordless when
   I turn me to the Word to pray. Amen.

To my Guardian Angel

Beauty and form's singular absence
Has embarrassed me before the Power
Who made all loveliness. In the hour

When the Fall's result, dark ugliness,
Shakes my body, you, Angel, come,
Solid and familiar as a nanny in the room.

Thank you, Angel, for your presence
During all the vile indignities
That accompany body's dis-ease.

You hold the beauty of the images
Which make all creation sacrament,
Even this. Now there is no embarrassment.

Sustained by your stern confidence
In the holiness of all created things
I rest within the comfort of your wings.

Silence is dangerous.
We never permit it.
Our vocabulary may not be large
But there is no question that we put it
to constant use.
That's what things are for:
to be used. And used.
And used.
Who knows?
If we didn't talk and chatter from morning
till night (it doesn't matter
whether or not anybody listens; that's
not the point),
Words might start using us.
We never allow silence.
If sometimes it catches us unaware,
I am the first to screech across it
And shatter it to echoing fragments.
You never can tell:
if I listened to the silence
I might discover
that I am real.

Someone has altered the script.
My lines have been changed.
The other actors are shifting rôles.
They don't come on when they're expected to,
and they don't say the lines I've written
and I'm being upstaged.
I thought I was writing this play
with a rather nice rôle for myself,
small, but juicy
and some excellent lines.
But nobody gives me my cues
and the scenery has been replaced
and I don't recognize the new sets.
This isn't the script I was writing.
I don't understand this play at all.

To grow up
is to find
the small part you are playing
in this extraordinary drama
written by
somebody else.

The children say the tree must reach the ceiling,
And so it does, angel on topmost branch,
Candy canes and golden globes and silver chains,
Trumpets that toot, and birds with feathered tails.
Each year we say, each year we fully mean:
"This is the loveliest tree of all." This tree
Bedecked with love and tinsel reaches heaven.
A pagan throwback may have brought it here
Into our room, and yet these decked-out boughs
Can represent those other trees, the one
Through which we fell in pride, when Eve forgot
That freedom is man's freedom to obey
And to adore, not to replace the light
With disobedient darkness and self-will.
On Twelfth Night when we strip the tree
And see its branches bare and winter cold
Outside the comfortable room, the tree
Is then the tree on which all darkness hanged,
Completing the betrayal that began
With that first stolen fruit. And then, O God,
This is the tree that Simon bore uphill,
This is the tree that held all love and life.
Forgive us, Lord, forgive us for that tree.
But now, still decked, bedecked, in joy arrayed

For these great days of Christmas thanks and song,
This is the tree that lights our faltering way,
For when man's first and proud rebellious act
Had reached its nadir on that hill of skulls
These shining, glimmering boughs remind us that
The knowledge that we stole was freely given
And we were sent the spirit's radiant strength
That we might know all things. We grasp for truth
And lose it till it comes to us by love.
The glory of Lebanon shines on this Christmas tree,
The tree of life that opens wide the gates.
The children say the tree must reach the ceiling,
And so it does: for me the tree has grown so high
It pierces through the vast and star-filled sky.

THE WINTER IS COLD,
IS COLD

The winter is cold, is cold.
All's spent in keeping warm.
Has joy been frozen, too?
I blow upon my hands
Stiff from the biting wind.
My heart beats slow, beats slow.
What has become of joy?

If joy's gone from my heart
Then it is closed to You
Who made it, gave it life.
If I protect myself
I'm hiding, Lord, from you.
How we defend ourselves
In ancient suits of mail!

Protected from the sword,
Shrinking from the wound,
We look for happiness,
Small, safety-seeking, dulled,
Selfish, exclusive, in-turned.
Elusive, evasive, peace comes
Only when it's not sought.

Help me forget the cold
That grips the grasping world.
Let me stretch out my hands
To purifying fire,
Clutching fingers uncurled.
Look! Here is the melting joy.
My heart beats once again.

Here at the time of a newer love's beginning
I see your body suddenly anew;
Each known and tempered touch, each sense and scent,
The strong and vulnerable and infinitely dear
Feel of the flesh that clothes your living bones
Wakens my body in the old and true response
Seen once again as miracle. To see you thus
As I have always seen you, but sometimes unaware,
Is unexpected grace. There is no part
Or portion that I do not love, but now
It is the human part, the fallen flesh
That wrenches me with startling pain and joy.
These bodies that will move to death, to dust,
Made, in an act of extraordinary grace
An explosion of light, a gift of life.
Now each expression that we make of love
Makes life anew, our lives a single life,
The two made one. In tenderness and play
We light the dark, and in this joyous game
We keep alight our candle's living flame.

Cold as charity, the saying goes:
I read it just now and it struck with the chill
Of the wind blowing in from the frozen river.
Cold as charity: the reluctant giver
Of love, the miser of self, cannot fill
Even himself with warmth. How the wind blows!

If I stand here in the cold I shall die
In this street of corpses and the grey near-dead.
Stone hands give out reluctant charity
And no one notices the wild disparity
Of the brilliant sun high overhead
Almost stilled by the clouds' chill cry.

My clothes keep out the heat of the sun!
I strip, I run from street to street
Chasing the distant sound of laughter,
Running, leaping, dancing after
The singing joy, my unshod feet
Glorying in the sun-warmed stone.

Naked, vulnerable, growing warm,
I meet another runner, arms spread wide
In loving and hilarious greeting.

The sun comes closer to light this meeting,
And shares our joyfulness as we stride
Laughing, exulting through wind and storm.

Nothing is everything to give,
A smile, a listening ear, a kiss,
Body and blood. Quick! Come and dine
On a crust of bread and the dregs of wine;
Never a feast was finer than this!
Come, eat and drink, unfreeze and live.

Body renewed and heart unfurled,
Love's banner blazes throughout the town
To twilight fear by law condemned,
To dayspring's joy by love redeemed.
Cold selfishness and dark be gone!
Burn, charity, and light the world!

Please, ma'am, my references are ample.
A small group of our family has always done domestic
    service.
Look at this recommendation; just a modest sample.
I know: my distant cousins make you nervous.

But think! I can replace all those machines in your
    residence.
You call that a stove! Well, just watch *me* boil water.
May I borrow that apron, please, and the kettle? Have no
    hesitance.
Watch. I spout a little flame. Fear not, I'll never eat your
    daughter.

I haven't fancied female flesh for years.
A touch more fire. See there? The kettle's boiling.
No, I'm a vegetarian now, eat modestly, make children
    laugh, dry tears,
Need little sleep, am not afraid of toiling,

Will save you fuel on your central heating.
I'm handy at making beds and sterilizing dishes.
These dusty rugs my tail is excellent at beating.
My disposition's sweet, and I grant wishes.

On winter nights when your feet are icy cold
I make a delightfully cozy foot warmer,
Can adjust my thermostat for young or old.
If burglars come I am a superb alarmer.

I guarantee I'll give you satisfaction.
Madam, I'm hurt! Unaccustomed to such dealings!
I cannot understand your rude reaction.
Remember that a dragon, too, has feelings.

If I can learn a little how to die,
To die while body, mind, and spirit still
Move in their triune dance of unity,
To die while living, dying I'll fulfill
The purpose of the finite in infinity.
If God will help me learn to die today,
Today in time I'll touch eternity,
And dying, thus will live within God's Way.
If I can free myself from self's iron bands,
Freed from myself not by myself, but through
Christ's presence in this simple room, in hands
Outstretched in holy friendship, then, born new
In death, truth will outlive the deathly lie,
And in love's light I will be taught to die.

O God, within this strange and quickened dust
The beating heart controls the coursing blood
In discipline that holds in check the flood
But cannot stem corrosion and dark rust.
In flesh's solitude I count it blest
That only you, my Lord, can see my heart
With passion's darkness tearing it apart
With storms of self, and tempests of unrest.
But your love breaks through blackness, bursts with light;
We separate ourselves, but you rebind
In Dayspring all our fragments; body, mind,
And spirit join, unite against the night.
Healed by your love, corruption and decay
Are turned, and whole, we greet the light of day.

When I was younger
Christmas was clearer
Magic was stronger
Santa Claus nearer.
He came from the North Pole
With reindeer wild
Bearing his soul
For the young Christ-child,
And toys and baubles
His elves had wrought
To take away troubles
And set them at naught.
An angel flew by him
To sit on the tree
And cherubs did cry him
And glory was three.
But now I am older
And Santa's a vagrant
On a street colder,
More crowded, less fragrant
Of pine cones and holly
And loving and laughter.
There's naught left but folly
And the bitter taste after.

I stand on a corner
Ringing a bell,
A red-suited mourner
Staving off hell
With a cupful of pennies
To throw on the table
Oh where and oh when is
The child in the stable
Coming to bring us
The tears that are mirth?
Come, angels, sing us
The death that is birth.

It was better in the jungle.
There I could imitate
the sound of dawn.
I could speak with the voice
of many tongues
and even if I didn't understand
I was still, in a sense,
an interpreter.
I could call with the song
of setting stars.
I could whisper with the leaves
before rain.

It is not the cage
that prisons me.
I, who live by mimicry,
have become made
in the image of man.

Good Samaritan

She comes on at night,
older than middle-aged, from the islands,
to answer the patients' bells
to see if it's worth disturbing an overworked nurse.
At first she was suspicious, cross,
expecting complaints and impositions,
soon tender and gentle,
concerned about requests for help with pain,
coming in (without being asked)
with a blanket if it turned cold,
hoping, as she said goodbye
at the night's end, for a good day.
This morning she rushed in, frantic,
please, please could she look for the money
she had lost somehow, tending patients,
forty dollars that was not even hers.
She had kept it, in time-honored tradition,
in her bosom, and it must have fallen out
when she was thinking of someone else's needs.
She scrabbled in the wastebasket,
in the bedclothes, panted from room to room,
returned to mine with a friend. We said,
"Close the door, take off your clothes, and see
if it isn't still on you somewhere."

She did, revealing an overworked body,
wrinkled, scarred; found nothing; had to leave.
She's off now, for a week. I'll never know
if she found it or not; will remember
her kindness and her panic. O God,
here, as so often, I cannot help.
Let me not forget she is your child
and your concern makes mine as nothing.
All I can do, and this I do, is love, is pray.

There's a hole in the world.
I'm afraid I may fall through.
Someone has died
Was
Has gone
Is where?
Will be
Is
How?
This is neither the first
Nor the only time that space has opened.
We are riddled with death
Like a sieve.
The dark holes are as multitudinous
As the stars in the galaxies,
As open to the cold blasts of wind.
If we fell through
What would we find?
Show me
Let me look through this new empty space
To where
The wind comes from
And the light begins.

The waves, the tides, the ocean: all in tune.
Raised from the sea my pale and ancient hand
Sprays benedictions from my silver wand.
How tender now the blessing of the moon.

Raised from the sea my pale and ancient hand
Absolves all creatures of the sea and dune
(How tender now the blessing of the moon)
The birds, the shellfish, water things, and land,

Absolves all creatures of the sea and dune,
The soaring dolphin by pure moonbeams fanned,
The birds, the shellfish, water things, and land.
Across the stars the wind sweeps out its tune.
On the white whale small flecks of silver stand
Caught by the light from soaring fountain spewn.
Across the stars the wind sweeps out its tune
For all my creatures, sky, and sea, and land.

CONFESSION SHORTLY BEFORE THE FORTY-EIGHTH BIRTHDAY

Here I am, beyond the middle middle,
According to chronology,
No closer to solving cosmic or private riddle,
No further from apology
For clumsy self's continuing ineptitude,
Still shaken by the heart's wild battering.
Intemperate passions constantly intrude;
I cannot keep small hurts from mattering,
Am shattered when met with mild irritation,
Need reassurance, feel inadequate and foolish,
Seek love's return, bump into abrogation,
Am stubborn beyond the point of being merely mulish.
So am I saved only by the strange stern power of silence,
The disciplined joy of work and rule
Inner and outer imposed, steel cold. The violence
Of the freezing wind sustains the heart. So this poor fool
Is fed, is nourished, forgets then to be concerned with rust;
Repentance, too, is turning, if towards dust,
And gratitude sings forth in adoration
Of the one who touched and healed the halt and lame
With the aweful, blissful power of his spoken Name.

INDEX
OF FIRST LINES